I was sick and you visited me:

Ministering hope in time of need

Mike Mellor

©Day One Publications 2016
First printed 2016

A CIP record is held at the British Library

ISBN 978-1-84625-496-3

Published by Day One Publications, Ryelands Road, Leominster, HR6 8NZ

☎ 01568 613 740
FAX 01568 611 473
email—sales@dayone.co.uk
web site—www.dayone.co.uk

Cover designed by Rob Jones, Elk Design
Printed by TJ International

To my dearest wife, Gwen, and our daughters,
Laura, Heidi, Vicki and Rebecca,
for their love, encouragement and patience.
How often through the 'busy' years the words
of Song of Songs 1:6 could regrettably have been
mine: 'my own vineyard I have neglected.'

ENDORSEMENTS

I'm delighted with this book and will recommend it as essential reading right across the leadership of my church family—for staff team, PCC and fellowship group leaders. I found it pastorally wise and practical, theologically utterly faithful and balanced, while at the same time filled with humanity and humour. It could only have been written by a man who has had decades of experience. It's my book of the year—and that's not just because it's so short!

Rico Tice, Associate Minister, All Souls Church, London, and co-author of Christianity Explored

It is not a fashionable ministry. However, periods of illness are times when God's people particularly need sensitive individual care from their church. Mike Mellor's book gives a brilliant blueprint to follow in this vital area of loving service. To neglect visiting the sick is to neglect Jesus himself (Matt. 25:43). To give one-to-one attention to his suffering people both encourages them and pleases the Lord.

Dr John Benton, Pastor, Chertsey Street Baptist Church, Guildford, and Editor of Evangelicals Now

Here is practical and pastoral wisdom for an important but often neglected task. Mike Mellor gives clear biblical direction and shares from years of valuable personal experience. The result is helpful without being prescriptive, and simple without being trite.

Graham Beynon, Pastor, Grace Church, Cambridge, and Director of Independent Ministry Training, Oak Hill College, London

The Bible clearly states in Ephesians 4:11–14 that God gave 'the apostles, the prophets, the evangelists, the shepherds and teachers, to equip the saints for the work of ministry, for building up the body of Christ, until we all attain to the unity of the faith and of the knowledge of the Son of God, to mature manhood, to the measure of the stature of the fullness of Christ, so that we may no longer be children, tossed to and fro by the waves and carried about by every wind of doctrine, by human cunning, by craftiness in deceitful schemes' (esv). This is one of those tools that anyone ministering could use to train and equip the saints for an effective ministry to those in need. It could be easily used to teach, instruct and disciple others for ministry. Mike Mellor's book will not be just another book on your shelf; it will be one of those resources you will refer to and use in ministry frequently. Caring for the body of Christ is not a luxury for a few but a mandate from Scripture for those he has assigned to oversee the flock.

Dr Charles Edward Boswell, Senior Pastor, Immanuel Baptist Church, Wichita, Kansas

In an age when church leaders are often portrayed as 'coaches' of the team, it's easy to lose sight of them as 'carers' of the flock. In a book that will take you an hour to read but a lifetime to absorb, Mike Mellor has done us a service in helping to redress the balance. Drawing on thirty years of pastoral experience he reminds us of the privilege of sharing with others in their weakness. Setting the visiting of the sick in the context of Judgement Day, he reminds us that this ministry is never about us: it is ultimately about the power of the gospel and the grace of Jesus experienced now in weakness and to be displayed one day to the glory of God. Whether or not you're a pastor, read this book and look for opportunities to do what it says. In doing so, you will be both blessed and a blessing!

Richard Underwood, Pastoral Ministries Director, Fellowship of Independent Evangelical Churches (FIEC)

ACKNOWLEDGEMENTS

My sincere thanks go to those whom over the years I have had the privilege of visiting in their time of need—most of whom are now fully healed, happy and 'home'—and who have been such a blessing to me, much more than my words could ever convey.

My thanks also go to the following:

To Bill James for his more than generous Foreword and helpful suggestions.

To my close friend Matt (not his real name), who gladly agreed to 'bare his soul' by providing an Appendix to help those seeking to serve any who struggle with mental illness in any of its many manifestations.

To Louise Morse of the Pilgrims' Friend Society for her Appendix and gracious guidance as we seek to be of comfort to those suffering with dementia.

To Mark Roberts of Day One for his faith in me, suggesting I attempt such a demanding subject.

To Suzanne Mitchell for her 'eagle-eyed' editing and welcome counsel.

Finally, to 'the Father of compassion and the God of all comfort' who is able to work through cracked and leaky 'clay pots', such is his desire to bless our suffering world.

CONTENTS

FOREWORD   **8**

PREFACE THE RETURN OF THE KING   **10**

INTRODUCTION A BEAM FROM HEAVEN   **12**

1 WHO SHOULD VISIT, AND WHY?   **14**

2 A VARIETY OF SITUATIONS   **24**

3 HOSPITALS, HOSPICES AND RESIDENTIAL HOMES   **34**

4 EVANGELISTIC SICK VISITING   **40**

5 WATCH AND PRAY   **46**

6 HEALING   **52**

7 A FRESH VISION OF GOD   **58**

8 SOME PRACTICAL POINTS   **70**

9 JOYFUL IN HOPE   **76**

APPENDIX 1 THE 'EACH OTHER / ONE ANOTHER' VERSES OF THE NEW TESTAMENT   **79**

APPENDIX 2 MINISTERING TO THOSE WITH MENTAL ILLNESS: A PERSONAL VIEW   **82**

APPENDIX 3 VISITING THOSE SUFFERING WITH ALZHEIMER'S OR DEMENTIA   **87**

APPENDIX 4 JAMES 5:14–16: HEALING AND CHURCH ELDERS   **91**

FOR FURTHER HELP AND INFORMATION   **94**

ENDNOTES   **95**

FOREWORD

When you are sick, who would you like to visit you at home or in your hospital bed?

Mike Mellor would be at the top of my list. He is a brother full of warm encouragement. He knows what it is to experience dark times in his own life, so is able to sympathize with our struggles. He brings cheer and comfort. But, more than anything else, he is a man who will bring us into the presence of the Saviour.

Times of sickness can be dark, when gloom and depression grip our souls. We feel alone, and perhaps are filled with fears about our condition or about the future. We need to hear words of reassurance that the Lord will never leave us nor forsake us, that his love will never fail, and that he is working out his good purposes for us even in the darkest days. We need someone to pray for us, and to pray with us.

Times of sickness can also be times of spiritual growth and close fellowship with the Lord. At the moment of our greatest weakness we cling with greater urgency to Christ, desiring his presence and his smile. We are conscious of the fragility of our mortal life, and we focus more clearly on our heavenly hope. The apostle Paul boasted that it was at times of his greatest weakness that God's strength was made known. It is in the furnace of affliction that our faith is refined and purified. Sometimes our fellowship with those who visit us in times of sickness is richer and deeper than at other times. Those who are not yet Christians can be more open to speaking of spiritual and eternal realities.

What an important ministry it is, then, to visit the sick, and what a privilege to speak of Christ to those who are suffering! Yet sometimes we are uncertain of ourselves and how we might serve in this way. Mike Mellor helps us by sharing his wisdom, accumulated over years of evangelistic and pastoral ministry. We are offered practical help on how to minister Christ, and how to express the love of the church family. This is not just a work for pastors or church officers, but something in which all might engage.

May the Lord use this little book to help us be an encouragement to those who are sick, to show our love and concern, and, most of all, to point them to the Saviour.

Bill James
Pastor
Emmanuel Church
Leamington Spa

PREFACE: THE RETURN OF THE KING

Heaven and earth have disappeared. Judgement seats are set in place. The King of the ages appears in all his heavenly splendour and takes his throne. The time has come for commendation and condemnation. He turns to those on his right, blesses them, and then invites them to share in his glorious eternal inheritance. As if that were not enough, he then, before an assembled heavenly multitude, publicly thanks them for their practical kindnesses performed in his name during their time on earth. Among his words of commendation are these: 'I was sick and you visited me' (Matt. 25:36, ESV).

Amid that vast assembled throng are the beaming faces of those *you* had visited! But now they are barely recognizable. No grey pallor. No look of confusion or fear. No pained expressions now. Not the slightest trace of sorrow or sadness.

A visit which at the time you thought inconsequential or unappreciated proved to be for the eternal glory of the Saviour and an everlasting joy to yourself. Any previous dark thoughts of time wasted in serving the sick now seem absurd in the light of such recognition and appreciation.

The aim of this book is simply threefold: firstly, to remove any lurking sense of duty we may feel when visiting those in their time of weakness and need; secondly, to give practical advice on how to be the greatest earthly blessing to our frail fellow sufferers as together we travel this often painful pathway through life; and thirdly, that whether 'professionals' or 'laypeople' we will be convinced that this a ministry all can—no, all *must*—exercise!

Forgive me if in these pages I refer to myself more than you find comfortable. My aim is simply to draw upon over thirty years' experience and put 'flesh and blood' on our visiting efforts. You will discover on numerous occasions that this is a 'how *not* to' rather than a 'how to' book!

Mike Mellor
West Moors
Dorset

INTRODUCTION: A BEAM FROM HEAVEN

She was frail as a sparrow, with legs like pencils, and ill-fitting teeth that barely kept up with her mouth as she spoke. But when I asked how she was as she lay in her bed, Gracie's china blue eyes twinkled mischievously as she beamed and chirped, 'I'm packed and ready to go, Pastor!' And indeed she was, and go she did, as a few days later the Lord gathered up another of his jewels. It had been my immense privilege on my visits to seek to make her transition a little more comfortable.

I used to frequently receive the same message: 'Gracie's fallen again!' I knew the cause of the fall before I called on her, of course. Those legs were just not built for speed and had no chance of keeping up with her Usain Bolt-like sprinting ambitions. However, I lost count of the times I returned from visiting her thinking the same thought: 'Who exactly ministered to whom there?' Once more I would be reminded of the eternal dimension to this work of 'visiting the sick', and the blessing that God grants to those who go in Jesus' name.

Bible teacher and author Warren Wiersbe rightly states that 'Ministry takes place when divine resources meet human needs through loving channels to the glory of God.'[1] We all no doubt feel our utter weakness and inadequacy when it comes to thinking how we could possibly be of any real benefit or blessing to someone in pain or discomfort. We naturally function better on those bright days when the sun is shining and the air is filled with a sweet fragrance; not so much when all seems dark, the air stale, and when pain is etched upon the face of the one we are visiting. But 'A friend loves at all times, and a brother is born for adversity' (Prov. 17:17); and so, in our felt weakness and uncertainty, we go in faith to be someone's friend, brother or sister in that person's time of need.

My prayer is that through this book a window might be opened into the sick room for a beam from heaven to shine in upon that troubled scene; that as we visit in Jesus' name we might have deeply engraved upon our hearts that what we are doing is pleasing to our great God and Saviour; and that visiting the sick, rather than being performed out of mere duty, will be seen as the most uplifting, humbling, joyful, sanctifying and satisfying of all Christian ministries.

In the pages that follow I have aimed to be as practical as possible. Above all else, it is my desire that we might glimpse a vision of the immense privilege that is ours as we seek to follow in the footsteps of the Saviour who poured out his heart in ministering to the sick, and that we might look to him to 'meet human needs through loving channels to the glory of God'.

Who should visit, and why?

IN THIS CHAPTER

Who should visit the sick? →

Making sense of sickness →

Bringers of hope →

Chapter 1

Duty makes us do things well, but love makes us do them beautifully.

–Phillips Brooks

Who should visit the sick?

PASTORS

You are a busy, conscientious pastor with a firm view on the primacy of preaching. You have a biblical conviction that you must 'give [your] attention to prayer and the ministry of the word' (Acts 6:4). That is right and true, and yet there is something disturbing about the servant of God who informs his church that he sees his calling as preaching to the flock but not visiting them.

There is something that happens within the heart of the pastor when he visits the sick that gives a dimension to his pulpit ministry which could be gained in no other way; a dimension which, if missing, causes the preaching to be 'sound' and yet to have a distant, metallic ring about it. It is a cutting indictment— yet containing too much truth to shrug off—that some men love preaching more than those to whom they preach. May that never be true of you, dear pastor.

It was said of Robert Murray M'Cheyne, whom many would look to as the model pastor, that 'He would visit the sick and grieving, often for many consecutive days, praying with them, reading Scripture, and encouraging them in their walk. At the end of one such full day he wrote, "O how sweet to work all day for God, and then to lie down at night under His smiles."'[1] This no doubt was one of the reasons that contributed to his unique power in the pulpit and his influence among the people under his care. In this respect M'Cheyne provides us with a much better pastoral pattern than the much revered twentieth-century pastor A. W. Tozer.

Tozer was one day on his way home from speaking at a

conference when, finding himself near the hospital to which one of his elders had been taken, he said to his driver, 'That's not far out of our way—let's visit him.' When Tozer came to the man's bedside the poor man froze and, turning to his wife, asked, 'Are you and the doctors hiding something from me? The pastor's here! Am I really that ill?'[2]

It is always good to remind ourselves that 'the best of men are men at best' and that we should imitate the strengths not the weaknesses of great men we admire.

ELDERS

It has been encouraging in recent years to see a recognition of the importance of setting apart as elders men within the fellowship (with the necessary gifts, of course) to govern jointly Christ's church as a pastoral team.

For those of us who have witnessed the sad outcome over the years of good men who have burnt themselves out, nobly perhaps but unbiblically, by a 'one-man' mentality, this is a welcome return and can only be of blessing to both pastor and people. To be sure, it is important to recognize that there will be a 'first among equals', a man who is equipped with particular gifts and who is due financial support and care (1 Tim. 5:17)—this man we fondly call 'the pastor'. Yet to expect him to carry the burden of shepherding the flock single-handed is both unreasonable and impractical, especially in our context of visiting the sick. And of course, pastors are also sheep and themselves stand in need of shepherding.

You may work out your own system in your church concerning the 'who' and 'how' of visiting those who are unwell, but of course you first need information. It is surprising how many in the church expect the elders to possess a psychic gift which enables them to know when they are sick! One simple yet effective way for churches that have mid-week homegroups is for the members to keep on the alert for any within their group who are unwell. They can contact the homegroup leader, who in turn can alert the pastor/elders regarding anyone requiring a visit. This also helps drive home the vital message that as the body of Christ, we 'should have equal concern for each other. If one part suffers, every part suffers with it' (1 Cor. 12:25–26).

Deacons

A deacon should never be seen as one merely 'taking care of the fabric of the church'—that is, taking care of the 'practical' matters while the elders take care of the 'spiritual'. In the early church, Stephen—generally recognized as the first church deacon to be set apart—was 'full of faith and of the Holy Spirit' (Acts 6:5): surely just the kind of person you would like to visit you when you are sick! Deacons are well placed to coordinate provision for the inevitable practical needs of those who are sick, have just given birth or who are in any kind of difficulty. The provision of lifts, meals and visits falls within this remit— and this is in addition to pastoral visits from the eldership. Another significant advantage in having deacons visit is that some churches have women in the role, which works well for visiting women especially.

Church members

We live in an increasingly individualistic and self-centred culture, and sadly many even within the church seem to be seeking freedom from any commitments that may impede their 'free-spirited' agenda. However, the Scriptures teach plainly that there can be no such thing as a 'Lone Ranger' Christian. All who claim to be looking to Christ as Saviour are interconnected as members of one body, with Christ as their Head (Rom. 12:5; Eph. 4:15–16). This is the reason why the King will say on that day, '… whatever you did for one of the least of these … you did for me' (Matt. 25:40). When Saul maliciously persecuted the church, he was actually persecuting Christ (Acts 9:4), and when we minister to one of the body, we minister to the Head. The New Testament is packed with 'one another' verses (see list in Appendix 1) that forcefully remind us that we each have a duty to lovingly care for one another. Even the busiest may find a way to encourage when hearing of one who is unwell. Letters, cards, telephone calls, assurance of prayer—all are apt if visiting is not possible or appropriate at that time. Love always finds a way.

No boundaries

The loving concern and compassion we are to show in visiting the sick is to be without any limitations or boundaries of church, colour, class, sexual orientation, belief or non-belief. Perhaps the best-known and best-loved of the Lord's parables is that of the Good Samaritan. Jesus left us no 'wriggle room', expecting us to be frontier-breakers, ministering to those who might consider us as enemies with an overflow of grace and mercy that comes from heaven itself. Who is my neighbour? Everyone outside the square foot of earth I occupy!

Why visit the sick?

Making sense of sickness

Without doubt the most popular question put to the Christian—and it may come in various forms—is, 'If there is a God, why does he allow suffering and sickness?'

As valuable as a comprehensive theology of sickness and suffering might be, it is outside the remit of this book. However, it might be helpful to put a little framework around our subject by taking a brief look at the root cause of the trauma and sadness we encounter whenever we visit a person at a time of distress. I believe that only the Scriptures provide a satisfying reason for why the world in which we live is one of great beauty and yet, at the same time, great ugliness, and of how we can experience such lofty delights and also such overwhelming sorrows: heaven and hell existing side by side on one small planet.

In the beginning

This world has not always been as it is today. We are told that at the birth of the universe God looked upon all that he had made and declared that it was 'very good' (Gen. 1:31). That perhaps is the greatest understatement of all time! He looked and saw a beautiful, pristine world working in perfect harmony. Perfect love flowed between God and man, and between the first man and woman. The earth produced perfect fruit, and the animal kingdom knew nothing of 'the food chain'. War and cruelty were unheard of. Joy and life, not pain and death, filled the air. But it was short-lived.

The entrance of sin

Many would insist that science, not the Bible, provides us with the answers to life's big questions, especially when looking at the origins of our world. The 'how' question is given much attention, but the 'why' question is usually ignored. In our sophisticated age many snigger at the thought of a couple's eating fruit as the explanation for our world's ills, but God records for us in his Word the exact reason *why* our world is racked with pain and misery. Every tear that has ever been shed can be traced back to that one act of rebellion in the Garden of Eden. We are told that 'sin entered the world' (Rom. 5:12), and catastrophic consequences along with it. This world and mankind would never be the same again. Not only would the physical universe be affected, but immediately fear, guilt, self-love and a thousand other things flooded into the hearts of the first humans.

Curse instead of blessing

All because of that fatal choice this world lies under God's curse rather than his blessing. As Adam was the representative head of the human race, he brought down the whole species with him in his fall. 'Sin entered the world through one man, and death through sin, and in this way death came to all men, because all sinned' (Rom. 5:12).

The world is still reeling from the effects of that wilful act. The sentence was pronounced: 'Cursed is the ground because of you' (Gen. 3:17). If only weeds were the sole evidence of this disastrous fall! But the whole of nature seems to cry out in pain; in fact, it is 'groaning as in the pains of childbirth right up to the present time', the apostle Paul explains (Rom. 8:22). At that split second sin entered the world, the entire cosmos changed and became 'out of joint', marred. So to this day, sickness and sadness, disease and death cast their dark shadow over the happiest moments of every human being in this life. Sickness is no respecter of persons; there is no one who can escape its grasp.

C. S. Lewis, the twentieth-century academic and writer, explained why so many have difficulty reconciling suffering with a God who is all-wise, loving and omnipotent:

> The problem of reconciling human suffering with the existence of a God who loves is only insoluble so long as we attach a trivial meaning to the word 'love' and look on things as if man were the centre of them. Man is not the centre. God does not exist for the sake of man. Man does not exist for his own sake. 'Thou hast created all things, and for thy pleasure they are and were created' (Rev. 4:11).[3]

Whether or not we agree with the Christian explanation for suffering, as a human race we are united in our pain and driven by compassion to encourage our fellow strugglers through this earthly pilgrimage. But it is the Christian alone who is equipped and qualified to bring hope to others in the fullest sense.

BRINGERS OF HOPE: THE GREAT REVERSAL

It is into this dark, depressing situation that people who know their God enter, bringing light and hope because they know that the last word is not with sickness and death!

How utterly hopeless all would be if God had left us in this predicament! But he is 'the compassionate and gracious God, slow to anger, abounding in love and faithfulness' (Exod. 34:6) and has mounted the greatest of rescue missions to save those he lovingly created in his own image. Far from being remote and unconcerned, God has himself entered this suffering world in the person of Jesus Christ—significantly a *suffering* Saviour who is called the second or 'last Adam' (1 Cor. 15:45–46) simply because he came to reverse the curse, that is, to succeed where our first parent failed, bringing blessing in place of the curse.

The resurrection of Jesus declares to a troubled world that there is One who has conquered sin, sickness, sorrow and death. There is no one but the Christian who has such a message of hope as this; no one who is better qualified and more motivated to lovingly and confidently draw alongside the sufferer!

LIFE IS PRECIOUS

We minister in a culture in which, because of the aggressive atheistic evolutionary agenda, people have been taught from the cradle that humans are merely a random 'bag of chemicals', made for no real purpose and of no real worth. They have been robbed of an education that teaches them of a loving, personal Creator and that they are each a unique 'one-off', made in the Creator's image and infinitely precious.

Professor Richard Dawkins' advice to any woman who should become pregnant with a baby with Down's syndrome was, 'Abort it and try again. It would be immoral to bring it into the world if you have the choice.'[4] His words are the alarming yet inevitable consequence of pro-choice as opposed to pro-life.

But all life is precious and deserves our noblest efforts. The care of human beings in life and in death must be a priority that we handle with divine wisdom and according to the divine pattern. Belief in a loving, personal Creator will inevitably affect our views on how we treat the unborn and the elderly, and it is no surprise that immense battles are presently being fought in the areas of abortion and assisted dying.

A CERTAIN FUTURE

Although we live in a world which, if able to speak, could only utter a 'groan', we look forward to that glorious day when God will liberate the whole of creation which presently is in 'bondage to decay' (Rom. 8:21–23). 'Then will the lame leap like a deer, and the mute tongue shout for joy' in the 'new heaven and … new earth, the home of righteousness' (Isa. 35:6; 2 Peter 3:13). We can comfort those who love Christ with the certain hope that a day is coming when God 'will wipe every tear from their eyes. There will be no more death or mourning or crying or pain, for the old order of things has passed away' (Rev. 21:4). And for those who do not know Christ, we can point them to him! He invites them, 'Come to me, all you who are weary and burdened, and I will give you rest. Take my yoke upon you and learn from me, for I am gentle and humble in heart, and you will find rest for your souls. For my yoke is easy and my burden is light' (Matt. 11:28–30).

EQUIPPED FOR THE JOB!

It is plain to see how God has fully equipped us for this incredibly important work. We have a tender heavenly Father who sends us into this broken world he so loves. We have a Saviour who, by his death and resurrection, provides all we need in order to be messengers of forgiveness, comfort and hope. And we have the Holy Spirit who empowers us and provides all the compassion, strength and wisdom we need for the task. Clearly, we have no excuse *not* to go!

A variety of situations

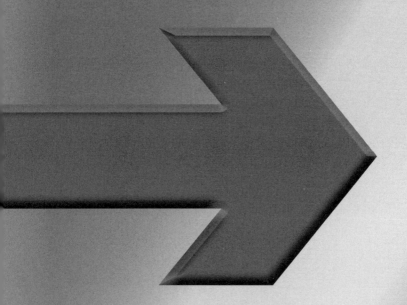

IN THIS CHAPTER

Being tough and tender →

Applying ourselves to different situations →

Chapter 2

I've heard there are troubles of more than one kind;
some come from ahead, and some come from
   behind.
But I've brought a big bat. I'm all ready, you see;
now my troubles are going to have troubles with me!

–Dr Seuss

Tough love?

You will be relieved to learn that we will not be turning much to Theodor Seuss Geisel for help in this area of visiting the sick, but in a work which requires much tenderness and compassion it is true that there is an element of warfare that calls for grit and determination. We need to be both tender and tough: tough in our tenderness and tender in our toughness. This is a ministry that can be extremely draining emotionally, and if we allow our emotions to rule us we will not be the help we need to be to those whom we visit. Added to that, we need to be adaptable and fully aware that a 'one size fits all' approach to visiting will never work.

For that reason, throughout this book I recount a selection of real-life scenarios in which I have found myself; each has thrown me upon the kindness of God for wisdom, discernment and empathy. It is essential that when we visit those who are sick, the very last thing we convey is that there is something mechanical about our time spent with them. Also, those we visit should be aware, not so much that *we* have called, but that *Another* has been present and has ministered to them and provided them with what they actually need, which may not necessarily be what they thought they wanted. There will be occasions when our visit might produce a 'godly sorrow [that] brings repentance that leads to salvation and leaves no regret'

(2 Cor. 7:10). Unlike any secular visitor, we seek to minister with eternity ever in view.

Faith and wisdom

Each visit is unique and we need to fight every inclination to slip into 'religious mode'—our prayers for the person and his or her situation being hollow, perfunctory or token. We must approach every person and occasion prayerfully, seeking to know how we should minister. What is this person's greatest need? Is it healing? Is it, for example, perseverance, encouragement, correction or direction? We must leave those we visit with an assurance that we have lifted them to God in our prayers and have left all in his loving care.

THOSE IN NEED OF ASSURANCE

The strongest saint is never far from moments of near despair. We need a constant awareness that the most mature of saints can be assailed by doubts and fears, and in fact will be a special target of the enemy of our souls when in a weak condition physically or mentally.

I was a newly converted Christian and had gone to visit a godly mature saint. Before trusting Christ, Gwynn had been a professional boxer in South Wales. He was now a radiant elderly believer who for many years had been fighting the world, the flesh and the devil and had encouraged me to join him in open-air preaching! For this reason, when I went to visit him in hospital I was staggered to discover that he was doubting his salvation. As a rookie in the faith it was a useful lesson for me that the godliest believer can be seriously assaulted by the enemy of our souls when he or she is ill, and can stand in need of another 'soldier' to draw alongside and remind him or her of the promises of God—which those of us in good health would consider the natural verses to turn to in times of doubt.

THOSE WHO ARE A LITTLE 'CRANKY'

There are those we seek to encourage who are consistently crotchety! They are undoubtedly the Lord's dear sheep, but for some reason, whether it is the result of a diet that produces excessive acid reflux or their being most happy when most snappy, whenever we seek to minister to them we always leave with the feeling that our visit has been a complete failure.

Harry was always a challenge for me. Although 'under the weather', he would sit in his chair with a small table at his side, upon which he had his Bible open (a King James almost the size of an old pulpit Bible). After listening to his complaints—a few regarding his health, but most to do with the church—I would read some Scripture (albeit in a 'condemned' version) and then seek to speak a few words in season, after which I would pray. It was never a comfortable time for me, yet strangely enough, in his own way—and carefully disguised—Harry came to appreciate the visits of his young pastor and we grew fond of each other. Well, I certainly grew fond of Harry anyway, and was glad to learn yet another lesson: that visiting is never about us or about how we 'feel'. It is one more opportunity to humble ourselves while seeking to be a blessing to others—whether we are appreciated in this life or not. We will meet Harry a little later concerning his wife who was diagnosed with a terminal illness.

THOSE IN CONSTANT PAIN

No one likes pain, yet we all have to endure it to some degree. However, there are some who have it continually, hour after hour, day and night, year after year. What on earth have we to say to such sufferers when we know so little of what they experience?

I used to visit Mary in her house that looked across a valley in South Wales. She had a condition that had caused her bones to become so brittle that she could not be moved without them being broken and she sat day and night in her wheelchair. What could have been for me a daunting and depressing experience was actually the very opposite. I never saw her without a smile upon her face and a word of encouragement upon her lips. She drank up the words of encouragement read from the Scriptures and we prayed for God to pour his grace upon her one more day, until that day when he would take her home and she would 'leap like the deer'.

There was no need for me to try to explain what God was doing; she simply took God at his word when he says, 'My thoughts are not your thoughts, neither are your ways my ways' (Isa. 55:8).

THOSE WITH MENTAL ILLNESS

'Mental pain is less dramatic than physical pain, but it is more common and also more hard to bear. The frequent attempt to conceal mental pain increases the burden: it is easier to say "My tooth is aching" than to say "My heart is broken."'[1]

The very phrase 'mental illness' is potentially a loaded expression and can cause alarm bells to ring and immediately convey the idea of extreme behaviour on the part of those who suffer with it. For years, mental illness has been a taboo subject in society, but thankfully now—either because of the increasing number of testimonies of high-profile public figures who suffer, or because of the all-too-frequent tragic deaths of globally famous celebrities—the problem seems to have been brought out into the open. Unfortunately there are still those within our churches who, while recognizing that of course Christians can have *physical* illnesses, at the same time deny the reality and problem of *mental* illnesses which a staggering number of believers battle with bravely and silently on a daily basis. When it comes to visiting a believer who suffers with some form of mental illness—whether it be, for example, depression, panic attacks, phobias, bipolar or an eating disorder—we must realize that we may need to firmly advise him or her to seek medical

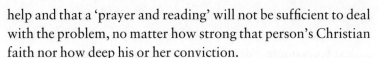

help and that a 'prayer and reading' will not be sufficient to deal with the problem, no matter how strong that person's Christian faith nor how deep his or her conviction.

I used to visit James in his home on a regular basis. He would always be the same, in a constant state of sadness and on the verge of tears. James loved the Lord and the Scriptures, but he remarked to me tearfully, 'No matter where I turn in the Scriptures, even though it might be a wonderful promise, I feel that God is condemning me.'

Passionate and cheerfully infectious British evangelist Roger Carswell has shared frankly his battles with depression in a helpful website article, reminding us that even great saints throughout Scripture and church history had their struggles in this area:

> Charles Spurgeon suffered depression after seven people died in a stampede when someone cried out 'fire' in one of his crowded worship services. William Cowper, who suffered from manic depression, attempted suicide for the third time the day after he wrote the hymn 'God Moves in a Mysterious Way'. Elijah, Jeremiah, David and Job were all familiar with the struggles of depression.[2]

We all battle with some form of human frailty and must avoid seeing mental illness as an embarrassment to be avoided or hushed up. The difficulty is trying to discern in our visits just where and how we may best be of help. Appendix 2 gives further guidance concerning this complex area.

THOSE WHO ARE TERMINALLY ILL

There can be no greater challenge than to visit one who is shortly to leave this world.

I received a phone call to say that Beryl had been diagnosed with cancer. It was making rapid progress through her body and she and her husband, Harry (whom we met earlier), were given the timescale of a matter of months. Although Harry (as we have already seen) was reliably cranky, he and Beryl were a devoted couple—devoted to the Lord and to each other. The months leading up to Beryl's death, although filled with sorrow and uncertainty, were at the same time a period of joy and hope, an experience that has been one of the greatest privileges of my life.

Knowing her time was short, Beryl wrote a tender, loving 'pastoral' note from her hospital bed to all her close family, most of whom were unconverted. She spoke of how she looked around her in the ward with great compassion and yearned for those who could look only to a few empty earthly pleasures for comfort while she was filled with joy at all she would soon enjoy because of Jesus.

The day came when Beryl was no longer conscious of her surroundings, but dear Harry continued with his daily practice of reading the Scriptures and then holding her hands while he prayed—after all, he was her personal pastor. On the final day, I observed Harry ministering to his wife. As he held her hands, Harry, in his charming cockney accent, turned to me and remarked, 'Ain't she beautiful!' I looked at Beryl and saw a pale, gaunt, dying old lady. But Harry didn't; he saw his beautiful bride whom he had loved and cherished through the years and now was committing into the hands of the Saviour who had laid down his life for her and who was now about to take her home.

The great encouragement for us who seek to visit the terminally ill is this: we go in the name of the One who is the Resurrection and the Life.

THOSE WITH DEMENTIA

Dementia is still a mystery in many ways. Alzheimer's disease is the leading cause of dementia, followed by vascular dementia. There are many other causes.

According to the National Institute on Aging (NIA)

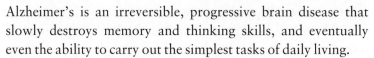

Alzheimer's is an irreversible, progressive brain disease that slowly destroys memory and thinking skills, and eventually even the ability to carry out the simplest tasks of daily living.

Dementia is a brain disorder that affects communication and the performance of daily activities—the loss of cognitive functioning, such as thinking, remembering and reasoning.

Relatives will often speak of having 'lost their loved one' before he or she dies. It is a tragic thing for anyone to observe in those whom they knew in their 'former glory'. 'Grief is living with absence, and grief is the major component of the dementia caregiver burden of post-bereavement psychological distress,' says Louise Morse, Media and Communications Manager for the Pilgrims' Friend Society.[3] It is also painful when seeking to visit and minister to those suffering with dementia.

Daniel is a friend and retired pastor. A warm, cheerful, outgoing man, fervent in his life and service, he was sadly diagnosed with Alzheimer's not long after he retired from the pastorate. We started to notice the slow but steady descent—the earlier stages of slight confusion when reading the Scriptures or praying in a meeting, through his not being able to find his car and eventually being told he was no longer able to drive, on to the point when he needed continual care and was taken into a residential care home. At this point our visits became increasingly difficult. Daniel still remained an active man and, even when I sat to talk, he would jump up and walk about. However, we take the Holy Spirit with us, and it is an encouragement to note evidence of his touching the inner essence of a person with comfort and even joy.

We need to be especially aware of the importance of visiting dementia sufferers. 'Loneliness of the soul is such a sad facet of dementia. Dementia sufferers need people more than [those suffering with] any other kind of illness,' adds Louise Morse.[4] Appendix 3, 'Visiting Those Suffering with Alzheimer's or Dementia', contains helpful tips from Louise Morse.

THOSE WHO ARE ELDERLY AND HOUSEBOUND

The elderly and housebound are a group who are vulnerable on a number of levels. The body is failing and they are having to cope with all kinds of aches, pains and perhaps illnesses. Loneliness can be a real issue. They live with a sense that they are a burden to family, friends and church. Also, it's only going one way! Veteran evangelist Billy Graham, quoting actress Bette Davies and now speaking from experience, writes, 'Old age is not for cissies!'[5]

When visiting them we need to remind these saints of their worth to God—and to us. For surely there is no more beautiful sight under the heavens than a man or woman who, like Enoch, has walked with God for years.

Don and Nancy were in their nineties. In their younger days, in their 'spare time' they had ridden all over South Wales on a motorbike giving out tracts and speaking about Christ. But now things were very different. As I entered their small flat, all was still. I would find them perched together on the sofa like a couple of lovebirds. Due to a medical condition which meant they could eat no fat, they both looked pale, drawn and emaciated. In an age which merely pays lip service regarding care and respect for the elderly, they would be considered to have lacked 'quality of life'. But that would have been a massively foolish conclusion to reach. I observed at the side of their sofa a pile of missionary prayer letters, magazines and Christian books. Old and frail as they were, their fingers were on the pulse of what God was doing in the church and in the world! After praying with them I would leave praising God and praying for myself, that I too might one day grow to be as old and as useful to the kingdom as Don and Nancy. So far only the former request seems to be being granted.

We cannot remind these saints too much just how precious they are to their God and to the church family, and that their presence is greatly missed in the fellowship. To reinforce this, it is good if we able to take communion with them in their home on occasions (see below) and perhaps arrange for them to receive a regular copy of the church bulletin/magazine to help them keep abreast of things. They need constant reassurance that, despite their felt weakness and all the messages this world gives to the contrary, their future is very bright! 'The path of the righteous is like the first gleam of dawn, shining ever brighter till the full light of day' (Prov. 4:18). No one is nearer that dazzling meridian light than those frail elderly yet faithful believers who have fought the good fight, finished the race, kept the faith and now are 'ripe for glory'. Let us do all we can to make their transition as smooth as possible, that they may finish their course with joy.

Visiting with communion

You will no doubt have your own way of sharing communion with those in the fellowship who through illness, being confined to a care home or otherwise through no fault of their own are deprived of attending the normal meetings when the church gathers around the Lord's Table. Our pattern during my time at Hope Church, Ferndown, was quite simply to have a minimum of two elders or an elder and wife visit. It can of course be more meaningful to those who perhaps have felt cut off or deprived of fellowship if a small group of warm-hearted believers from the church accompanies you.

Hospitals, hospices and residential homes

IN THIS CHAPTER

Preparing for the unexpected →

Permission required? →

Practicalities →

Prayer back-up →

A Scout is never taken by surprise; he knows exactly what to do when anything unexpected happens.
–Robert Baden-Powell, founder of the
Boy Scout movement

Preparing for the unexpected

You may not have had the benefit of being a Scout in your youth, but Baden-Powell wisely saw the need for youngsters to be adaptable in life and the various situations it inevitably throws at us. Adaptability is certainly an important quality when it comes to visiting the sick. Visits to hospitals, residential homes and the like are normally more challenging because the setting is usually more formal and less private, and the hours of visiting are more restrictive. But positively, because of this, they can often prove to lead to wonderful unplanned opportunities (or perhaps more accurately, divine appointments), and for this reason we need that essential pastoral qualification—R.F.A., *Ready for anything!*

Permission required?

If we are visiting one of these institutions within the stated visiting hours, naturally no permission is required; however, if we are seeking to visit outside these hours we will need to phone ahead and first ask if it is possible to visit out of hours, and then give the reason why we are requesting this exception (pastoral reasons, family circumstances, etc.).

MINISTERIAL FAVOUR

Times have changed, and these are days when, by and large, a secular mindset rules. The days when ministers were seen as essential and therefore respected leaders in the community are almost gone (the USA may be behind the UK in this respect); nevertheless there still remains some acknowledgement of the importance of the minister's role and value for 'religiously minded' people. (If ever there was a time and place for the clerical collar, this is it!) Thankfully, there is a desire within healthcare to provide holistic care for patients, but Christian pastors can no longer presume upon receiving special treatment and often must be prepared to stand in line with the imam, rabbi, white witch or anyone else when it comes to privileges in visiting being granted.

MORNINGS

Morning visits are normally out of bounds for most institutions due to doctors' rounds, cleaning and so on. (Close family, however, are always looked upon with sympathy and exceptions are usually made in special circumstances.)

Practicalities

- Ensure your cell phone is turned off!
- Be calm, relaxed and cheerful. The patient is in an abnormal situation and will be tense or embarrassed at the best of times when people visit, no matter how welcome you might be. Convey your relaxed attitude through warmth of voice, eyes and smile. 'A cheerful heart is good medicine' (Prov. 17:22), and this can be true for patient and visitor alike! (More on this in Chapter 8.)
- Make the visit short and let any family present at the time know that that is your intention.
- Try to choose the best time to read the Scriptures and pray. This is not always easy if other visitors are there. Don't read too much! (Pray for the Holy Spirit to guide you before you arrive.) Ideally, read and pray just before you depart, as we want to bring something of God to those we visit and leave them with a sense of *his* presence, not *ours*. Luke records in his Gospel how

'Jesus himself drew near' (24:15, KJV). This surely is our deepest desire for all whom we visit.

- Remember there are others in the ward. If you are visiting a ward where there are patients in other beds, it can be the door to other opportunities! When reading and praying, I seek to do so in a voice that is natural but which can be heard by others in the ward. When saying 'goodbye' to 'my' patient, I cast an eye around the ward and smile, watching to see if there is any reaction from anybody else. If I sense there is, I approach the patient and ask how he or she is. If appropriate, I ask if that patient would like me to pray for him or her too. If able, I gently go a little further, being careful not to be pushy. I then leave a little tract or booklet 'I just happen to have in my pocket' for him or her to read. Often this opens a door for 'my' patient to continue the ministry!

Prayer back-up
While we should seek to undergird all that we are doing in our own personal prayers, it is essential that we have some mechanism in place so that we are able to contact other believers to pray for particular people or situations.

PRAYER CHAINS
It is helpful for a church to have a number of prayer chains—that is, groups of people on a list who have volunteered to be contacted when any pressing need arises. This can work in a number of ways. For example, there may be, say, eight people on a list. The person at the top of the list is always contacted first; he or she then phones person number 2 with the item for prayer, and person number 2 then phones person number 3—and so on, until all have been contacted. This may more effectively be executed via a text message notifying all the group simultaneously.

'INNER CIRCLE' OF PRAY-ERS

It is significant to note that, although the Lord Jesus gathered twelve disciples around him, he seemed to have his 'inner circle' of Peter, James and John that he drew near him on certain occasions (Matt. 17:1; Mark 14:33). There are times when for various reasons it is not appropriate to spread the request for prayer too widely concerning a sick person, but there still remains the urgent need for prayer back-up. At times like this we need to have our 'inner circle' of faithful and trusted pray-ers who will uphold both the sick person and ourselves as visitors.

THE LOCAL CHURCH

Although lacking the flexibility and intimacy of smaller groups, the local church is the 'power house' provided by God to bring heaven's blessing down upon this sad world. It is important, therefore, that we not only make known any requests for prayer, but that we also report back any changes, updates and answers to prayer.

Evangelistic sick visiting

IN THIS CHAPTER

Tender-hearted and eternity-minded →

Death-bed conversions →

Taking opportunities →

Chapter 4

We have one business on earth—to save souls!
–John Wesley

I'm sure you won't misunderstand me when I use the term 'evangelistic sick visiting': I am in no way seeking to encourage the predatory 'scalp-hunting' mentality that is seen too often among the cults and false religions of our day. Rather I want us to never lose sight that in all our visits to those struggling with failing bodies or minds, there is a more important eternal issue involved. In a day when the emphasis is put upon caring for individuals 'from the cradle to the grave' and ensuring that people 'die with dignity', we as Christians must have ever before us that great day when the King will come in his heavenly glory and gather before him for judgement all who ever lived. There will be two groups, and only two groups—the righteous and the unrighteous, the saved and the unsaved, the forgiven and the unforgiven—and only two destinations: '... they [the wicked] will go away to eternal punishment, but the righteous to eternal life' (Matt. 25:46).

Overflow
All we do and say must flow from a heart steeped in the love of God. Our every thought, word, look and action must course from that same love and grace which we ourselves have experienced in the past and continue to receive on a daily, even moment-by-moment basis.

The apostle Paul reminds us of who God is and how his nature should be communicated through us: he is 'the Father of compassion and the God of all comfort, who comforts us in all our troubles, so that we can comfort those in any trouble with the comfort we ourselves have received from God' (2 Cor. 1:3–4).

Courage
When it comes to ministering to one who is not far from entering

eternity, it is no time to hold back the truth of each of us having to appear before our holy God and Judge; even though the situation might be far from ideal we need to prayerfully 'grasp the nettle'. It is here again that we need to ask God for those dual qualities of toughness and tenderness—and how we need the Spirit's aid in this area perhaps above every other! How precious a thing it is at such times to be able to speak of a kind and merciful Saviour who is willing and able to save all who call upon him in their time of need, no matter how late in the day they have left eternal matters to be resolved (Matt. 20:1–16; 23:43). Often a good way into a spiritual conversation is to ask, 'Do you have a personal faith that can help you through this time?' or some other question that acts as a bridge from the natural to the spiritual realm.

Sensitivity

Few have had the tender compassion for men and women held by Robert Murray M'Cheyne; his view of eternity produced in him the toughness and tenderness mentioned above that are so vital in our visiting: 'Sometimes he witnessed death-bed conversions. Others resisted the Gospel, and it was amongst them that he displayed real courage and manliness. He showed the utmost sensitivity and graciousness to the dying, but refused to allow himself the luxury of professional detachment. The gospel had to be communicated to the dying faithfully, robustly and clearly.'[1] Concerning his personal visits it was said of M'Cheyne that 'His voice, and his very eye, spoke tenderness; for personal affliction had taught him to feel sympathy for the sorrowing.'[2]

We, of course, may be lesser men and women than the heroes of the past we so delight to read of, yet let us never forget that the God who equipped his saints of old is well able to open doors for us and provide all that we need for each particular occasion. We must beware falling into the sin of Moses, who, when sent by God, ventured from the holy ground of faith and humility and trespassed into the forbidden territory of unbelief and pride, incurring God's anger (Exod. 4:13–14).

Death-bed conversions?

Puritan preacher and writer William Guthrie, commenting on the thief on the cross who repented in his dying hours, remarked that in all the Scriptures 'there is but one instance of a deathbed conversion—one that none may despair, and but one, that none may presume'.[3]

Pam, the wife of one of the church elders, was a GP working with cancer patients. Not only was she much loved and highly respected by all, but also she had the heart of an evangelist, and whenever the opportunity arose she would ask a patient, 'Would you like a visit from my pastor?' On many occasions I was provided with a precious and natural opportunity to speak of Christ to those who knew that their days on earth were few.

On one of those occasions I was asked to visit a man who had been moved into a side ward of the hospital for his remaining time. I opened the door to see Ed, a large but gaunt man with a grey pallor. As we spoke, I couldn't help noticing that in his bedside cabinet was a huge tome about all the religions of the world. I guessed his thinking: 'I had better sort one of these out pretty quickly!' I took one look at the book and one look at Ed and thought to myself, 'He's not going to have time to finish it!' It is at moments like this that I thank God not only for the beauty and freeness of the gospel, but also for its simplicity. After explaining to Ed that he was loved by God, that it was not too late for him to get right with him and that Christ had done all that was needed, I gave him a simple tract, *Peace with God*, and then left.[4]

I called back a few days later, not knowing if Ed would be there or not. Slowly opening the door, I peered in and there was Ed—still grey and gaunt, but with an enormous smile and eyes aglow with joy! As I sat beside him he took my hand in his large hands and said excitedly, 'I want to tell you what has happened!' But I already knew. A greater Visitor than I had been there—and just in time, as within a few days Ed was gone. But his eternal destiny had been changed. Death-bed conversions may be rare, but they must be prayed for and expected when we visit.

Unconverted family members of Christians

We have in our churches those who battle on as the only believers in their families, and it is on our visits to these saints that we may have spiritual opportunities with these family members. Even at the risk of their having to endure a little embarrassment, discomfort or humbling, the fact that there is someone who cares and prays for one they love may in itself be a means of opening their hearts and minds to the gospel.

Betty was a sweet, faithful Christian married to Dilwyn, who was a good man, a paramedic, yet humanistic and atheistic in his outlook. He 'did his bit' for society and was 'pleased for Betty' that 'her religion did her good'. When I visited their home, Dil would usher me in to his wife then politely leave me to do the 'religious bit', while he moved on to more practical, manly matters. One couldn't help feeling wimpish as Dil, a broad-shouldered six-footer, left the room. However, I began to discern a gradual change in him after he was diagnosed with a life-threatening illness. This keen gardener would linger when I visited and make some comment on how there must be 'Someone behind the scenes' who gives life, makes thing grow and so on. As time passed, Dil would hover around then stay in the room as I read the Scriptures and prayed with Betty. My wife, Gwen, and I had them both round for dinner and a friendship developed—albeit a short one, as not long afterwards, a very ill man, Dil was taken into hospital. Even then I did not expect the call that was to bring the good news. 'Hello, Pastor!' chirped the excited voice on the telephone. 'Dil has come through!' My mind being elsewhere (in the middle of sermon preparation), I thought, 'Come through what?' 'He has trusted the Lord!' Betty qualified. I expressed how pleased I was, yet even as I put the phone down I was inwardly grappling with how God could be so gracious to someone who had not yet come to church on a Sunday! But 'come through' Dil most certainly did, as for his remaining weeks on earth he showed a genuine love and gratitude towards the One who had loved him and given his life for him. One factor that cannot be left out, however, is that Betty had prayed for her stubborn husband for over forty years!

Watch and pray

IN THIS CHAPTER

Watching ourselves →

Praying in the Spirit→

Let us ask for a fresh gift of the Holy Spirit to quicken our sluggish hearts, a new disclosure of the love of God. The Spirit will help our infirmities, and the very compassion of the Son of God will fall upon us, clothing us with zeal as with a garment, stirring our affections into a most vehement flame, and filling our souls with heaven.

–David McIntyre, *The Hidden Life of Prayer*

Watching ourselves

DRY

Do you remember the first time you were overwhelmed by the love of Christ? Do you remember when you were first struck by the fact that you were loved, not because of any good you could perform for God, but despite his knowing the very worst about you? Do you remember when that love compelled you to share it with others, whether in word or deed? Failing to continue in that way is what our risen Saviour calls 'forsak[ing] your first love' (Rev. 2:4). When in that state we have fallen into the trap of just 'doing' ministry, going from task to task machine-like. Our life has become dry and our hearts have become hard.

REFRESHED

Ideally, it is best not to allow ourselves to get to that point, and to heed the warning, 'Above all else, guard your heart, for it is the wellspring of life' (Prov. 4:23). But if it is too late, there is never room for despair: there is always a way back. 'Remember—Repent—Repeat,' says our Lord Jesus (see Rev. 2:4–5). Remember how things were, repent of how hard and dry you have become, and then do those things you used to do before you entered zombie-zone.

Take heart! Even the godliest and most zealous Christian can be reduced to this state—but it need never be final!

Christmas Evans was renowned as a zealous church planter and a remarkably powerful preacher in North Wales in the eighteenth and nineteenth centuries. Many new chapels were built, the money being collected on preaching tours which Evans undertook in South Wales. He was a lion in the defence of the gospel—and yet he awoke one day to the fact that he was merely 'going through the motions'. His testimony should be a tonic and encouragement for us all:

> I was weary of a cold heart towards Christ and his sacrifice and the work of his Spirit; of a cold heart in the pulpit, in secret and in the study. For fifteen years previously I had felt my heart burning within as if going to Emmaus with Jesus. On a day ever to be remembered by me, as I was going from Dolgellau to Machynlleth, climbing up towards Cader Idris, I considered it to be incumbent upon me to pray, however hard I felt in my heart and however worldly the frame of my spirit was. Having begun in the name of Jesus, I soon felt as it were, the fetters loosening and the old hardness of heart softening, and, as I thought, mountains of frost and snow dissolving and melting within me. This engendered confidence in my soul in the promise of the Holy Ghost. I felt my whole mind relieved from some great bondage. Tears flowed copiously and I was constrained to cry out for the gracious visits of God, by restoring to my soul the joys of his salvation and to visit the churches in Anglesey that were under my care.[1]

Praying in the Spirit

MIND THE RUT!

If you have travelled on the London Underground you will have

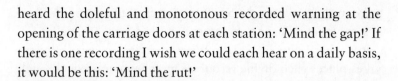

heard the doleful and monotonous recorded warning at the opening of the carriage doors at each station: 'Mind the gap!' If there is one recording I wish we could each hear on a daily basis, it would be this: 'Mind the rut!'

Auto-pilot praying

What could be worse when seeking to visit some needy soul with the aim of imparting spiritual life and bringing down blessing from heaven, than to intone a heartless perfunctory prayer for which you expect no answer? Even if that is an extreme example, it should serve as a reminder of how we need to speak from the overflow of hearts immersed in the love and grace of God. Hence the need to 'guard the heart', making sure that we are careful to be in fellowship with God and are actively seeking to keep our spiritual life fresh.

Praying in the Spirit

'I only evangelize when I get a fuzzy feeling,' offered a young man once when I was engaged in open-air ministry. I replied that, if I were to do the same, I would never evangelize! It is the same in any form of Christian ministry. After having done all we can to ensure we are 'alive', the fact remains that we are 'in the body', and while living in this sad fallen world we inevitably 'groan inwardly'—especially when engaged in ministering to the sick. It is because of this constant 'down-drag' that we need to go forth in faith with the assurance that 'God will meet all [our] needs according to his glorious riches in Christ Jesus' (Phil. 4:19) and will enable us to serve in a power far beyond our own—in the realm of the Spirit. I can certainly testify to this personally, as on many an occasion I have almost had to drag myself out, feeling as though I were wearing a pair of the weighted space boots given to astronauts! Yet, to my delight, something happened. The love and grace of God flowed through this unworthy clay pot for the blessing of a needy individual. We were in the realm of the Spirit, and everything changed. (And yes, sometimes I have even returned with 'a fuzzy feeling'!)

It is what I quoted Warren Wiersbe saying earlier: 'Ministry takes place when divine resources meet human needs through loving channels to the glory of God.'

EXPECTANCY

Surely the most challenging factor when it comes to praying for someone who is sick is, 'What exactly should I be praying for right now?' If the person is old and frail and knows the Lord, is it right to be praying for that person's healing? Or what if the person is young and has wandered far from God? Just what ought I to be praying for? Every situation is different, and it is for this reason we need a humble dependence upon our omniscient, all-wise God. The point is, however, that we always need to come with a spirit of faith and expectancy whenever we visit, and commit this dear soul to the One who cares for him or her much more than we ever could, and desires the best for him or her—whatever that might be!

Healing

IN THIS CHAPTER

What should we expect? →

Healing in Christ's atonement? →

The 'not yet' and the 'then' →

The fact of suffering undoubtedly constitutes the single greatest challenge to the Christian faith, and has been in every generation.

–John Stott, *The Cross of Christ*

Given the scope and aim of this book it is impossible to deal satisfactorily with the massive and vital matter of healing. But mention must be made, no matter how cursorily, simply because our view on healing will inevitably affect the way we visit and pray for those who are sick. Healing is always a thorny issue and we doubtless will all approach this subject from a variety of viewpoints.

The problem is rarely, if ever, '*Can* God heal?' but normally, '*Is it his will* to heal?'

Surely it is essential that we never, ever lose sight of the fact that God could break into the life and situation of the one we are visiting and completely transform it! We must never come in Christ's name without believing he may change or overrule a diagnosis and prognosis in a way which will confound the greatest and most respected medical practitioners. To do so would be to enter that sick room cloaked in unbelief and leave behind us an aura of doom with the one we had intended to be blessed by our visit.

On the other hand, having successfully avoided the quicksand of unbelief, we must beware of crashing onto the rocks of presumption, bringing a false hope and expectancy which may well prove to devastate rather than strengthen the faith of the one visited.

The danger of giving false hope

Joni Eareckson Tada has grappled with this thorny issue courageously and with astounding grace for nearly five decades as a quadriplegic. On more occasions than she would wish to recall, she has been told (even rebuked!) that if only she had enough faith she would be out of her wheelchair. She recalls how on one occasion, filled with faith, hope and expectancy, she was taken to the meeting of a famous healing evangelist. The atmosphere was electric and as the evangelist

> breezed onto the stage ... my heart raced as I prayed, 'Lord, the Bible says You heal all our diseases. I'm ready for You to get me out of this wheelchair. Please would You?' But the spotlight always seemed to be directed towards some other part of the ballroom where apparent healings were happening. Never did they aim the light at the wheelchair section where all the 'hard cases' were: quadriplegics like me, stroke survivors, children with muscular dystrophy, and men and women sitting stiff and rigid from multiple sclerosis. God answered. And again, His answer was no. After the crusade I was number fifteen in a line of thirty wheelchair users waiting to exit at the stadium elevator, all of us trying to make a fast escape ahead of the people on crutches. I remember glancing around at all the disappointed and quietly confused people and thinking 'Something's wrong with this picture. Is this the only way to deal with suffering? Trying desperately to remove it? Get rid of? Heal it?'[1]

The divine prerogative

The unmistakable bottom line is that God reserves the right to heal. Admittedly, it is a mystery to us as to why sometimes he does heal and sometimes he doesn't. However, we can rest in what we *do* know about God and his character: the fact that he is an all-loving, all-wise, kind heavenly Father who can be trusted totally, even though his ways are at times way beyond our comprehension—and satisfaction!

Joni concludes, 'Ah, there are many things that God has

revealed—things I do know and understand. But there are many more things he has not chosen to reveal, and may not reveal this side of heaven, and one of those things is why he sometimes steps in to heal one person and not another.'[2] Anyone who has followed the witness and ministry of this remarkable woman over the years will be forced to admit what a blessing her unhealed life has been to untold millions and should not find it too difficult to understand why God refused to grant her the release she must have longed for—and still must long for at times.

Healing in the atonement?

Much emphasis is placed in some quarters on there being a provision of healing in the atonement. Such an idea is promoted especially by Word of Faith Movement TV personalities, who lean heavily upon Isaiah 53:5: '… and by his wounds we are healed'. Even though such a viewpoint may be at the extreme end of the spectrum, its influence is enormous. It truly is not only a shallow but actually a cruel viewpoint that states, as many faith teachers do repeatedly in their widespread mantras, 'It is never God's will for you to be sick', or 'You cannot glorify God if you are sick.' This certainly is not the God of the Bible, nor of Joni Eareckson Tada. The early church father Augustine takes us to the heart of the issue when helpfully remarking, 'Job does not say, "The LORD gave, and the Devil took away," but, "The LORD hath taken away."'[3] Satan and sickness come unquestionably under the authority of the sovereign Lord, and if he fails to heal it is because he has a higher reason which most probably only eternity will reveal to the bewildered sufferer.

The 'not yet' and the 'then'

Many would not go as far as the Word of Faith proponents but they still seek to squeeze from Isaiah 53:5 that which goes beyond what was intended. To be sure, there is healing in the atonement.

On the cross, Christ dealt once and for all with the problem of sin and its devastating and far-reaching consequences. But only in heaven will we be free from the downwards drag of the sinful actions, words and thoughts that so distress us as believers. Only in heaven shall we be free from the curse of sickness our bodies and minds presently reel from. But that glorious day of total release will come—hallelujah! We need that true biblical faith in the God of miracles that has not the slightest doubt that 'nothing is impossible with God' (Luke 1:37) and yet does not waver if healing is denied, but rather clings tenaciously and lovingly to the One who cried in agony to his Father, 'Yet not as I will, but as you will' (Matt. 26:39). May the Lord grant us in each and every situation the ability to discern the 'not yet' from the 'then', that we may help those we visit to live for the glory of God whether in sickness or in health; and that we may provide them with every encouragement to 'shine ever brighter until the perfect day' (see Prov. 4:18), when all things will be made new, and pain and suffering will be no more.

> Therefore we do not lose heart. Though outwardly we are wasting away, yet inwardly we are being renewed day by day. For our light and momentary troubles are achieving for us an eternal glory that far outweighs them all. So we fix our eyes not on what is seen, but on what is unseen. For what is seen is temporary, but what is unseen is eternal (2 Cor. 4:16–18).

See also Appendix 4, 'James 5:13–16: Healing and Church Elders'.

A fresh vision of God

IN THIS CHAPTER

Restoring a right perspective →

Our spiritual medical chest→

It may be of use to keep an account when and where God has been pleased to manifest himself to our souls in a peculiar manner … 'Remember, O my soul! And never forget what communications of divine love thou didst receive at such a time, at such a place; tell others what God did for thee.'
–Matthew Henry on Ezekiel 1:1–3

Restoring a right perspective

Surely there can be no greater achievement after visiting a sick person than to have left him or her with a fresh vision of God. Perspective is one of the first things we lose when illness casts its dark garment over us. No matter how mature a suffering saint is or how theologically loaded, he or she will inevitably stand in desperate need of recapturing something of the reality of God, something of his glorious attributes—those characteristics of our God and Saviour that enable us to anchor our very soul to him during a time of crisis when the storm is raging and the waters are high. It is for this reason that as physicians of souls we carry with us our spiritual medical chest, the Scriptures. Naturally, we are only too aware that when a person is unwell his or her ability to concentrate is almost always at a low ebb, so we must think in terms of 'quality not quantity' as we prayerfully seek the Holy Spirit's help to guide us in reading the portion needed for each occasion. But although we may focus merely on one facet of our infinite God's being, we do so believing that a shaft of glory might shine into the life of this dear one, bringing a comfort far greater than that which any human word can produce.

You may gather and store your own supply of heavenly medicine from that vast chest; however, below I have listed God's attributes together with sample verses that may be used to drop divine comfort into the soul of a friend at a time when the voices of doubt and the devil may be loud and persistent and his or her greatest need is for truth to restore a battered faith. It is then that perspective may be regained and the sufferer may be able to once again see its beautiful child—Hope.

The love of God: pointing to the One whose very being is love

Zephaniah 3:17 The LORD your God is with you, he is mighty to save. He will take great delight in you, he will quiet you with his love, he will rejoice over you with singing.

1 John 4:9–10 This is how God showed his love among us: He sent his one and only Son into the world that we might live through him. This is love: not that we loved God, but that he loved us and sent his Son as an atoning sacrifice for our sins.

Jude 20–21 But you, dear friends, build yourselves up in your most holy faith and pray in the Holy Spirit. Keep yourselves in God's love as you wait for the mercy of our Lord Jesus Christ to bring you to eternal life.

The power of God: pointing to the One who is strong when we are weak

Isaiah 41:10–13 So do not fear, for I am with you; do not be dismayed, for I am your God. I will strengthen you and help you; I will uphold you with my righteous right hand. All who rage against you will surely be ashamed and disgraced; those who oppose you will be as nothing and perish. Though you search for your enemies, you will not find them. Those who wage war against you will be as nothing at all. For I am the LORD, your God, who takes hold of your right hand and says to you, Do not fear; I will help you.

Matthew 28:18–20 Then Jesus came to them and said, 'All

authority in heaven and on earth has been given to me. Therefore go and make disciples of all nations, baptizing them in the name of the Father and of the Son and of the Holy Spirit, and teaching them to obey everything I have commanded you. And surely I am with you always, to the very end of the age.'

Ephesians 3:20–21 Now to him who is able to do immeasurably more than all we ask or imagine, according to his power that is at work within us, to him be glory in the church and in Christ Jesus throughout all generations, for ever and ever! Amen.

The compassion of God: pointing to the One whose power is harnessed to infinite tenderness

Psalm 103:8–14 The LORD is compassionate and gracious, slow to anger, abounding in love. He will not always accuse, nor will he harbour his anger for ever; he does not treat us as our sins deserve or repay us according to our iniquities. For as high as the heavens are above the earth, so great is his love for those who fear him; as far as the east is from the west, so far has he removed our transgressions from us. As a father has compassion on his children, so the LORD has compassion on those who fear him; for he knows how we are formed, he remembers that we are dust.

Mark 6:34 When Jesus landed and saw a large crowd, he had compassion on them, because they were like sheep without a shepherd. So he began teaching them many things

John 11:35 Jesus wept.

2 Corinthians 1:3–5 Praise be to the God and Father of our Lord Jesus Christ, the Father of compassion and the God of all comfort, who comforts us in all our troubles, so that we can comfort those in any trouble with the comfort we ourselves have received from God. For just as the sufferings of Christ flow over into our lives, so also through Christ our comfort overflows.

The sovereignty of God: pointing to the One who controls all things, from the greatest to the minutest

Psalm 31:14–15a But I trust in you, O LORD; I say, 'You are my God.' My times are in your hands.

Psalm 115:1–3 Not to us, O LORD, not to us but to your name be the glory because of your love and faithfulness. Why do the nations say, 'Where is their God?' Our God is in heaven; he does whatever pleases him.

Revelation 19:5–9 Then a voice came from the throne, saying: 'Praise our God, all you his servants, you who fear him, both small and great!' Then I heard what sounded like a great multitude, like the roar of rushing waters and like loud peals of thunder, shouting: 'Hallelujah! For our Lord God Almighty reigns. Let us rejoice and be glad and give him glory! For the wedding of the Lamb has come, and his bride has made herself ready. Fine linen, bright and clean, was given her to wear.' [...] Then the angel said to me, 'Write: "Blessed are those who are invited to the wedding supper of the Lamb!"' And he added, 'These are the true words of God.'

The wisdom of God: pointing to the One for whom it is impossible to err

Job 42:1–3 Then Job replied to the LORD: 'I know that you can do all things; no plan of yours can be thwarted. You asked, "Who is this that obscures my counsel without knowledge?" Surely I spoke of things I did not understand, things too wonderful for me to know.'

Psalm 18:30–33 As for God, his way is perfect; the word of the LORD is flawless. He is a shield for all who take refuge in him. For who is God besides the LORD? And who is the Rock except our God? It is God who arms me with strength and makes my way perfect. He makes my feet like the feet of a deer; he enables me to stand on the heights.

Romans 11:33–36 Oh, the depth of the riches of the wisdom and knowledge of God! How unsearchable his judgments, and his paths beyond tracing out! 'Who has known the mind of the Lord? Or who has been his counsellor?' 'Who has ever given to God, that God should repay him?' For from him and through him and to him are all things. To him be the glory for ever! Amen.

The faithfulness of God: pointing to the One who can be trusted at all times

Deuteronomy 7:9 Know therefore that the Lord your God is God; he is the faithful God, keeping his covenant of love to a thousand generations of those who love him and keep his commands.

1 Corinthians 10:13 No temptation has seized you except what is common to man. And God is faithful; he will not let you be tempted beyond what you can bear. But when you are tempted, he will also provide a way out so that you can stand up under it.

2 Timothy 2:11–13 Here is a trustworthy saying: If we died with him, we will also live with him; if we endure, we will also reign with him. If we disown him, he will also disown us; if we are faithless, he will remain faithful, for he cannot disown himself.

The providence of God: pointing to the One who is directing all things towards his glorious eternal end

Genesis 50:18–21 His brothers then came and threw themselves down before [Joseph]. 'We are your slaves,' they said. But Joseph said to them, 'Don't be afraid. Am I in the place of God? You intended to harm me, but God intended it for good to accomplish what is now being done, the saving of many lives. So then, don't be afraid. I will provide for you and your children.' And he reassured them and spoke kindly to them.

Proverbs 16:9 In his heart a man plans his course, but the LORD determines his steps.

Acts 17:26–28 From one man he made every nation of men, that they should inhabit the whole earth; and he determined the times set for them and the exact places where they should live. God did this so that men would seek him and perhaps reach out for him and find him, though he is not far from each one of us. For in him we live and move and have our being.

The immutability of God: pointing to the One who is unchanging in his character and purposes

Psalm 18:1–2 I love you, O LORD, my strength. The LORD is my rock, my fortress and my deliverer; my God is my rock, in whom I take refuge. He is my shield and the horn of my salvation, my stronghold.

Hebrews 13:8 Jesus Christ is the same yesterday, today and for ever.

Revelation 1:8 'I am the Alpha and the Omega,' says the Lord God, 'who is, and who was, and who is to come, the Almighty.'

The mercy of God: pointing to the One who does not treat us as our sins deserve but delights to bless

Psalm 145:8–9 The LORD is gracious and compassionate, slow to anger and rich in love. The LORD is good to all; he has compassion on all he has made.

Titus 3:3–7 At one time we too were foolish, disobedient, deceived and enslaved by all kinds of passions and pleasures. We lived in malice and envy, being hated and hating one another. But when the kindness and love of God our Saviour appeared, he saved us, not because of righteous things we had done, but because of his mercy. He saved us through the washing of rebirth and renewal by the Holy Spirit, whom he poured out on us generously through Jesus Christ our Saviour, so that, having been justified by his grace, we might become heirs having the hope of eternal life.

Hebrews 4:14–16 Therefore, since we have a great high priest who has gone through the heavens, Jesus the Son of God, let us hold firmly to the faith we profess. For we do not have a high priest who is unable to sympathize with our weaknesses, but we have one who has been tempted in every way, just as we are—yet was without sin. Let us then approach the throne of grace with confidence, so that we may receive mercy and find grace to help us in our time of need.

The transcendence of God: pointing to the One who is totally above and independent of this material world

1 Chronicles 29:10–12 David praised the LORD in the presence of the whole assembly, saying, 'Praise be to you, O LORD, God of our father Israel, from everlasting to everlasting. Yours, O LORD, is the greatness and the power and the glory and the majesty and the splendour, for everything in heaven and earth is yours. Yours, O LORD, is the kingdom; you are exalted as head over all. Wealth and honour come from you; you are the ruler of all things. In your hands are strength and power to exalt and give strength to all.'

Isaiah 55:8–9 'For my thoughts are not your thoughts, neither are your ways my ways,' declares the LORD. 'As the heavens are higher than the earth, so are my ways higher than your ways and my thoughts than your thoughts.'

1 Timothy 6:13–16 In the sight of God, who gives life to everything, and of Christ Jesus, who while testifying before Pontius Pilate made the good confession, I charge you to keep this command without spot or blame until the appearing of our Lord Jesus Christ, which God will bring about in his own time— God, the blessed and only Ruler, the King of kings and Lord of lords, who alone is immortal and who lives in unapproachable light, whom no one has seen or can see. To him be honour and might for ever. Amen.

The grace of God: pointing to the One who showers favour upon those who deserve condemnation

2 Corinthians 12:8–9 Three times I pleaded with the Lord to take [the thorn in the flesh] away from me. But he said to me, 'My grace is sufficient for you, for my power is made perfect in weakness.' Therefore I will boast all the more gladly about my weaknesses, so that Christ's power may rest on me.

Ephesians 1:3–8 Praise be to the God and Father of our Lord Jesus Christ, who has blessed us in the heavenly realms with every spiritual blessing in Christ. For he chose us in him before the creation of the world to be holy and blameless in his sight. In love he predestined us to be adopted as his sons through Jesus Christ, in accordance with his pleasure and will—to the praise of his glorious grace, which he has freely given us in the One he loves. In him we have redemption through his blood, the forgiveness of sins, in accordance with the riches of God's grace that he lavished on us with all wisdom and understanding.

The omniscience of God: pointing to the One who has total knowledge of all things, whether visible or invisible

Psalm 139:1–6 O LORD, you have searched me and you know me. You know when I sit and when I rise; you perceive my thoughts from afar. You discern my going out and my lying down; you are familiar with all my ways. Before a word is on my tongue you know it completely, O LORD. You hem me in—behind and before; you have laid your hand upon me. Such knowledge is too wonderful for me, too lofty for me to attain.

Isaiah 40:27–29 Why do you say, O Jacob, and complain, O Israel, 'My way is hidden from the LORD; my cause is disregarded by my God'? Do you not know? Have you not heard? The LORD is the everlasting God, the Creator of the ends of the earth. He will not grow tired or weary, and his understanding no one can fathom. He gives strength to the weary and increases the power of the weak.

Matthew 10:29–31 Are not two sparrows sold for a penny? Yet not one of them will fall to the ground apart from the will of your Father. And even the very hairs of your head are all numbered. So don't be afraid; you are worth more than many sparrows.

The goodness of God: pointing to the One whose ways are perfect and trustworthy at all times

Deuteronomy 33:26–27 There is no one like the God of Jeshurun, who rides on the heavens to help you and on the clouds in his majesty. The eternal God is your refuge, and underneath are the everlasting arms.

Psalm 73:1, 21–26 Surely God is good to Israel, to those who are pure in heart … When my heart was grieved and my spirit embittered, I was senseless and ignorant; I was a brute beast before you. Yet I am always with you; you hold me by my right hand. You guide me with your counsel, and afterwards you will take me into glory. Whom have I in heaven but you? And earth has nothing I desire besides you. My flesh and my heart may fail, but God is the strength of my heart and my portion for ever.

James 1:17 Every good and perfect gift is from above, coming down from the Father of the heavenly lights, who does not change like shifting shadows.

Of course, the Gospels are packed with these attributes in flesh and blood form as they were manifested powerfully in the life and ministry of our Lord Jesus, the God-man, to whom we will inevitably turn in our visiting. The above sample of verses may nevertheless be of help in enabling us to remember to keep bringing the 'whole counsel of God' with us into this vital ministry.

Some practical points

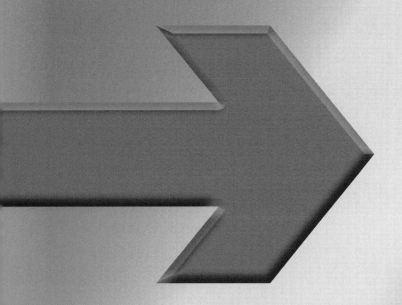

IN THIS CHAPTER

Body language: touch, eyes, voice →

Miscellaneous tips →

Protection from discouragement →

Chapter 8

**Your body communicates as well as your mouth.
Don't contradict yourself.**

–Allen Ruddock

Such is the glorious responsibility of this work of visiting the sick that one could be excused for wondering why God has not appointed angelic beings to bring the heavenly comfort that is needed at such times! The stark truth remains that he has commissioned frail flesh and blood to be his carriers of comfort. So, while doing all we can to ensure we are prepared spiritually in our visiting, it is also important to consider some further essential practical matters that, if neglected, may hinder the impact of our efforts.

Body language

We don't want to be over-conscious of our body language! We should seek always to be as natural as possible in every area of life—to be, as someone has put it, 'Natural in our spiritual life, and spiritual in our natural life.' That said, we are not disembodied spirits, therefore we dare not neglect the fact that much is conveyed to others through our physical being and that we ourselves are part of the message of good news we seek to carry and convey. 'A cheerful look brings joy to the heart, and good news gives health to the bones' (Prov. 15:30).

Touch

Touch is an area that always calls for discernment, but it is an especially important matter when we visit those who, in their condition of sickness, will perhaps be feeling most isolated, insecure, vulnerable and be standing in need of assurance and affirmation. Where the opposite sex is concerned physical touch will need particular care—and some cultures are less tactile than others—but let us bear in mind that we can still convey appropriate warmth as long as we 'Treat … older women as mothers, and younger women as sisters, with absolute purity' (1 Tim. 5:1–2). I was deeply saddened some years ago to learn of the fall of a young pastor whose moral failure could be traced back to his holding hands and praying with a young female church member he visited in hospital. But physical touch has the potential to do great good, and we need not be deterred because of incidents which are the exception. Perhaps the old adage 'If in doubt, don't' might serve us well in this instance.

EYES

Our eyes convey a great deal; they inform others whether we are happy or sad, bored or interested, relaxed or nervous. Hopefully, our body language will convey that we are genuinely glad to be visiting the sick person and that we consider it to be a sincere joy and privilege to be with him or her at that time, sharing in his or her plight. However, the reality might be that we are desperately tired, deeply worried about a personal concern or fearful of the condition of the one we have come to reassure. We therefore need to come with a prayerful dependence upon God that he will convey his love, assurance or sympathy through this poor earthen vessel. It is important we retain good eye contact that conveys that the one we have come to visit has our full attention. At the same time, we need to be aware that prolonged eye contact may appear intense, so in conversation it is good to occasionally look away and then back again.

It is surprising how many times the Gospel accounts mention Jesus not merely watching but 'looking' at people. Perhaps the most touching example is that of the encounter he had with a wealthy young man, who walked away from him. 'Jesus looked at him and loved him' (Mark 10:21). It would seem that it was the Saviour's look of love that broke the heart of the impetuous fisherman Peter (Luke 22:61–62). Let us pray that in our visiting ministry, our eyes will convey the warmth, grace and compassion of the God in whose name we come.

VOICE

Your voice, just like your thumbprint or DNA, is a unique gift and sets you apart from any other person. For this reason, be natural and avoid seeking to take another with you—your more spiritual, 'visiting' voice. (Spurgeon made fun of certain preachers who spoke in an unnatural 'parsonic' voice!) The sick person is in an unnatural enough situation, especially if in hospital, and will perhaps be desperate for some kind of normality. Be sure to speak loudly enough for the sick person to hear—but avoid shouting. (Of course, there is no option but to shout if he or she is hard of hearing and without a hearing aid!) God has given us voices that are capable of communicating a wide range of sounds and emotions. (Do you ever read the words of Jesus in the Gospels and think to yourself, 'I wonder how Jesus said that'?) So pray for the Holy Spirit to make your voice as well as the words spoken a means of blessing, especially as you read the Scriptures and pray.

We are carriers of hope into situations which are often dark and depressing; therefore, we must ever seek to 'overflow with hope' (Rom. 15:13) in the totality of our being.

Miscellaneous tips

- Don't talk about yourself (unless asked to do so—and then be brief and turn the subject back to the one you are visiting).
- Don't get involved in medical matters, commenting on treatment, and so on.
- Don't feed a complaining spirit.
- Don't be surprised if a mature saint acts out of character. Illness can do that.
- Don't stay too long and tire the patient (twenty minutes is about right in a normal situation).
- Don't pressure the patient to speak of spiritual matters. Let this happen naturally.

- Don't read too long a passage of Scripture.
- Don't have a lazy 'one size fits all' approach to your reading.
- Do be calm, pleasant, joyful and relaxed.
- Do be natural. You are not a robot, so there is room for appropriate emotion.
- Do seek (subtly!) to assess the sick person's spiritual condition, and minister accordingly.
- Do pray for the Holy Spirit to minister through you.
- Do read the Scriptures and pray at the *end* of your visit.
- Do remember to pray for the family and all concerned parties.
- Do remind the sick person that the church loves and prays for him or her.
- Do be aware of personal hygiene—bad breath, body odour, and so on.

Protection from discouragement

No matter how experienced you may be, entering situations of illness (physical, and especially mental) on a regular basis will inevitably take its toll.

- Seek to detect in yourself when things are starting to get to you.
- Be aware especially of times of tiredness.
- Don't unload your burden at the expense of your wife or family.
- Remember that you are not God. Don't carry weights he alone can bear. Remember that Jesus said his burden was light—and we are yoked with him (Matt. 11:28–30).
- Pray—not only for those people and situations you are concerned about, but also ensuring you cast your burdens upon the Lord (1 Peter 5:7).
- Keep your sense of humour in good shape. 'A cheerful

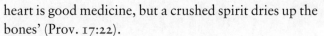

heart is good medicine, but a crushed spirit dries up the bones' (Prov. 17:22).

• Do something relaxing—sport, hobbies, a walk, a visit to the gym, DIY, even watch a silly DVD.

Keeping perspective is vital in all Christian ministry, but especially in this area. It is impossible to sustain constant tension, so maintain a healthy balance in your life, remembering that there is 'a time to weep and a time to laugh, a time to mourn and a time to dance' (Eccles. 3:4)—a time to minister to the sick and a time to relax.

Joyful in hope

IN THIS CHAPTER

Present hope →
More than conquerors →
In Jesus' name →

Chapter 9

If you are not allowed to laugh in heaven, I don't want to go there.

–Martin Luther

Future certainty

Whereas Puritan pastor/theologian/revivalist Jonathan Edwards summed up heaven as 'a world of love',[1] the great Reformer Martin Luther saw it as a world of joy. And how could it not be, when all traces of sin will have been removed and the redeemed shall rejoice with glorious new bodies in a perfect new creation! Happiness and praise will be our spontaneous and most natural response when we shall see and enjoy all that God has prepared for us.

Present hope

We are called to anticipate and enjoy this future certainty now, even though we 'groan inwardly' and 'wait eagerly for our adoption as sons, the redemption of our bodies' (Rom. 8:23). The reality is, however, that when illness throws its dark cloak over our lives, rejoicing in that prospect—no matter how temptingly it may be described—may be the very last thing we actually feel like doing, as heaven and all spiritual things seem so distant and unreal. It is here where those visiting may bring something of heaven with them, just as 'Saul's son Jonathan went to David at Horesh and helped him to find strength in God' (1 Sam. 23:16). We need to remind those who are ill or incapacitated that the day is certainly coming for the Lord's dear ones when pain, tears and frustration will be gone for ever and 'the lame [will] leap like a deer … Gladness and joy will overtake them, and sorrow and sighing will flee away' (Isa.35:6, 10).

More than conquerors

Whatever our condition as we navigate through the inescapable traumas of this troubled world, we have the choice of being either victims or victors. But surely it is in the lives and examples of those faithful *un*healed individuals that we see the unfathomable grace of God most powerfully declared and demonstrated.

Joni Eareckson Tada illustrates this beautifully through an incident that occurred while she attended a conference in Lausanne.

> On the last night our Issue Group, many of whom were disabled themselves, began to pray for healing for those who were ill or in pain. The Holy Spirit then led us to pray for all the nations and people groups that were represented in the room. The power of God's love and joy spilled over. After interceding the group suddenly began to dance, whether in wheelchairs, on crutches or on legs, in a holy chain of rejoicing in God's overwhelming love. The chain wove through the lobby and able bodied participants of the Forum joined in or cheered as God was glorified in the praises of His earthen vessels.[2]

In Jesus' name

How unparalleled, then, is the privilege which is ours of visiting the sick, ministering in Christ's name! Only on the day the King returns shall we fully realize that it actually was the King himself we visited and ministered to.

APPENDIX 1. THE 'EACH OTHER / ONE ANOTHER' VERSES OF THE NEW TESTAMENT

1 '… be at peace with each other' (Mark 9:50).

2 '… wash one another's feet' (John 13:14).

3 'Love one another' (John 13:34).

4 '… you must love one another' (John 13:34).

5 '… love one another' (John 13:35).

6 'Love each other …' (John 15:12).

7 'Love each other' (John 15:17).

8 'Be devoted to one another in brotherly love' (Rom. 12:10).

9 'Honour one another above yourselves' (Rom. 12:10).

10 'Live in harmony with one another' (Rom. 12:16).

11 '… love one another …' (Rom. 13:8).

12 '… stop passing judgment on one another' (Rom. 14:13).

13 'Accept one another, then, just as Christ accepted you' (Rom. 15:7).

14 '… instruct one another' (Rom. 15:14).

15 'Greet one another with a holy kiss' (Rom. 16:16).

16 '… when you come together to eat, wait for each other' (1 Cor. 11:33).

17 '… have equal concern for each other' (1 Cor. 12:25).

18 'Greet one another with a holy kiss' (1 Cor. 16:20).

19 'Greet one another with a holy kiss' (2 Cor. 13:12).

20 '… serve one another in love' (Gal. 5:13).

21 'If you keep on biting and devouring each other … you will be destroyed by each other' (Gal. 5:15).

22 'Let us not become conceited, provoking and envying each other' (Gal. 5:26).

23 'Carry each other's burdens …' (Gal. 6:2).

24 '… be patient, bearing with one another in love' (Eph. 4:2).

25 'Be kind and compassionate to one another …' (Eph. 4:32).

26 '… forgiving each other …' (Eph. 4:32).

27 'Speak to one another with psalms, hymns and spiritual songs' (Eph. 5:19).

28 'Submit to one another out of reverence for Christ' (Eph. 5:21).

29 '… in humility consider others better than yourselves' (Phil. 2:3).

30 'Do not lie to each other …' (Col. 3:9).

31 'Bear with each other …' (Col. 3:13).

32 '… forgive whatever grievances you may have against one another' (Col. 3:13).

33 '… teach [one another]' (Col. 3:16).

34 '… admonish one another' (Col. 3:16).

35 'May the Lord make your love increase and overflow for each other' (1 Thes. 3:12).

36 '… love each other' (1 Thes. 4:9).

37 '… encourage each other …' (1 Thes. 4:18).

38 '… encourage one another …' (1 Thes. 5:11).

39 '… build each other up …' (1 Thes. 5:11).

40 'Encourage one another daily …' (Heb. 3:13).

41 '… spur one another on towards love and good deeds' (Heb. 10:24).

42 '… encourage one another' (Heb. 10:25).

43 '… do not slander one another' (James 4:11).

44 'Don't grumble against each other' (James 5:9).

45 '… confess your sins to each other' (James 5:16).

46 '... pray for each other' (James 5:16).

47 '... love one another deeply, from the heart' (1 Peter 1:22).

48 '... live in harmony with one another' (1 Peter 3:8).

49 '... love each other deeply' (1 Peter 4:8).

50 'Offer hospitality to one another without grumbling' (1 Peter 4:9).

51 'Each one should use whatever gift he has received to serve others ...' (1 Peter 4:10).

52 '... clothe yourselves with humility towards one another' (1 Peter 5:5).

53 'Greet one another with a kiss of love' (1 Peter 5:14).

54 '... love one another' (1 John 3:11).

55 '... love one another' (1 John 3:23).

56 '... love one another' (1 John 4:7)

57 '... love one another' (1 John 4:11).

58 '... love one another' (1 John 4:12).

59 '... love one another' (2 John 5).[1]

APPENDIX 2. MINISTERING TO THOSE WITH MENTAL ILLNESS: A PERSONAL VIEW

Matt is a close friend and a godly, gracious man who seeks to honour God, love the Lord Jesus Christ, be sensitive to the Holy Spirit and order his life day by day according to Scripture. Here he shares his personal insight into how best we can minister to those suffering with mental illness.

Greatly misunderstood

I am just one among many thousands who have to wrestle with mental illness on a daily basis. Historically, mental illness has been a stigmatized, maligned and largely misunderstood subject, and is frequently and erroneously conveyed as being synonymous with the sufferer being 'weak'. Having battled with a protracted mental anxiety-related condition (and subsequent depression), I have found the truth to be the opposite—that in fact, it takes great inner strength and fortitude to endure the darkest moments that a mental illness foists upon you. Rather than having a natural flow through life that many people enjoy, you seemingly can be fighting through every waking moment with little or no satisfaction for doing so. The subject of how this relates to the church and how the church should serve the mentally ill requires continued attention, wisdom and due caution.

The human brain is complex far beyond what we can coherently understand, and scientists/medical practitioners are in many respects only scraping the surface of how this wondrous organ functions. According to my limited research, the brain operates with the use of a myriad of biological chemicals referred to as neurotransmitters. In my own condition, I fundamentally lack sufficient quantities of one (or more) of these neurotransmitters and, as a result, I experience repetitive and involuntary anxiety. In various forms of mental illness, from clinical depression to anxiety disorders, the sufferer cannot help but experience the misery that comes with the condition. Praise be to God that there are medical/psychiatric advances that have allowed myself and countless others to live enjoyable lives despite having such biological dispositions to melancholy and/or anxiety. Based on my own experience, here are a few pointers that may aid those who attend to the needs of the mentally ill.

A wide spectrum of disorders

Firstly, mental illness covers a wide spectrum of disorders and forms of depression, with an even wider framework of causes for each case. With such a vast array of mental illnesses stemming from varying causes, it is important that sufferers seek help from the source that is best equipped to offer pointed treatment, namely, medical practitioners.

A few causation factors of mental illness are:

- The person may be subject to an entirely physiological issue such as a chemical imbalance in the brain. This was indeed the case with myself.
- The person could be feeling the weight of his or her conscience for something he or she has done wrong, whether it be habitual or a one-off event.
- The issue could be related to the person having been maltreated in some capacity in the past.
- There could be satanic oppression at work. We need to be very cautious to jump to conclusions in this regard, as so doing can serve to significantly confuse matters.
- There may be some form of post-traumatic stress syndrome resulting from a previous distressing experience or event.
- Even types of parenting can reinforce or produce a mental sensitivity that espouses mental imbalances, either immediately or later in life.

- The person may be harbouring bitterness or an inability
to forgive another.

This list is by no means exhaustive, but it can at least give a
feel for just how difficult it can be to determine the source of
mental illness, not least because a person's condition can be a
complex intertwined mix of many factors.

I have found from personal experience that the church is often
ill-equipped to deal effectively with the mentally ill—and in a
way, rightfully so, as it is not the primary responsibility of the
church to diagnose and treat those with mental illness. It can be
far more beneficial for a visitor to lend a listening ear and direct
the sufferer to seek mental help through a qualified professional.
The church/Christian visitor can aid in spiritual matters, but
where one enters the physiological/psychological realm, proper
assessment by someone who knows the intricacies of the human
psyche is required. The misdiagnosing of a physiological illness
as a spiritual matter can have dramatically negative effects on
the sufferer; we therefore need to operate with due caution,
wisdom and vigilance when coming to conclusions about the
sufferer's plight.

Some resulting effects of mistaking the physiological as
spiritual could be:

- Causing the sufferer to come under condemnation he
or she finds great difficulty in emerging from, as he or
she cannot treat the problem following the erroneous
advice that has been given.
- Shaking the person's faith; he or she may feel a sub-
standard Christian and incapable of walking with God.
- Causing the person to have a warped view of God,
producing a Job-like thought process: that God is
an enemy, crushing him or her under an unbearable
weight. This can result in the sufferer becoming angry
or bitter towards God.
- Bringing the person under false guilt and the conviction

84

of having somehow sinned his or her way out of God's favour.
- Causing the person to embark on a long journey of leaving no spiritual stone unturned—yet without his or her receiving any answer or relief, leading only to prolonged despair.

This is an area where we may in all sincerity be seeking to help but may actually *worsen* the condition of one struggling with mental health issues. *It is vital to know when to advise the sufferer to seek medical help.* Having said this, Christians can of course be of enormous help and encouragement.

Practical tips for supporting the mentally ill

- Do not belittle the sufferer by labelling him or her as 'weak'. This can cause massive setbacks to the person's recovery. To live and cope with a mental illness can be unfathomably difficult.
- Empathy—or lack of it. If you have never had the form of mental illness you are encountering in another person, you probably cannot understand that person's suffering. If there is another person in the church with the same illness, it might be helpful to put the two in contact, so that someone with a first-hand understanding can help the sufferer. But even in this, caution needs to be exercised; while there may be some benefit, professional help is still the preferred and primary course of action.
- Be slow to speak and quick to listen. Ask questions and be prepared to listen to the answers. Be very cautious in offering any advice. Know your limitations and admit when something is out of your depth—then advise the person to seek professional help.
- Consider taking another person when visiting someone with mental illness, as the sufferer may not be in a

good state of mind or may be out of touch with reality. By having another person present, you reduce the potential of putting yourself in difficult or undesirable circumstances.

• Pray for God's wisdom in dealing with the person.

• Healing is possible but not guaranteed. Don't promise the sufferer anything, as this can prove soul-destroying to the sufferer if God chooses to do otherwise. The apostle Paul asked three times for his thorn in the flesh to be removed, but God refused as it was a vehicle of humility for him.

• Exercise caution and wisdom when dealing with the mentally ill at all times, as they can be fragile and are prone to hang on every word.

• Above all, continue to show love, compassion and patience. These qualities, together with the assurance of your prayers, are invaluable.

APPENDIX 3. VISITING THOSE SUFFERING WITH ALZHEIMER'S OR DEMENTIA

Pilgrims' Friend Society has published a most helpful pamphlet written by Louise Morse and Roger Hitchings. The following suggestions are listed below with their kind permission.[1]

Before you visit

1. Unless you know the person very well, find out as much as you can about them. They will have a personal history, which will include deeply held beliefs and values. Some phrases will be especially meaningful and comforting to them, and can act as triggers for good or for bad! Find out from the caregiver, or the carer in the nursing or care home, as much as you can about these.

2. Check whether or not they need a hearing aid, or spectacles, and make sure they have them available and use them.

3. If you are engaging in devotions, or any spiritual activity, use the version of the Bible and the types of hymns that they are familiar with. 'How Great Thou Art' is more meaningful to older people than the more modern 'How Great Is Our God', for example, and the old King James version than more modern translations. This is very important, as older memories stay intact longer than later ones—remember, your preferences are irrelevant! It is what they know and can relate to that matters.

4. Take notice of your background in the way you speak and pray. Some may prefer prayers read from *The Book of Common Prayer*, whereas some prefer spontaneous prayer. Reading familiar prayers can be a great comfort when someone is struggling with uncertainty.

5. Find out how they like to be addressed. First names

may well be acceptable, but let them decide, or ask their caregiver, who knows them best.

6. The sense of touch is very important to some people with dementia. Check with the caregiver or carer at the home. If the individual likes to hold hands, hold hands very gently, remembering the fragility of old age. Sometimes the individual likes to touch you—perhaps stroking your arm. Be sure you know in advance.

During your visit

1. Keep each session brief and direct.
2. Sit close, if appropriate, and maintain good eye contact—and a relaxed, friendly expression. People with dementia are particularly sensitive to body language and unexpressed emotion.
3. Speak clearly, and not too quickly.
4. Be consistent in all you do and say. Avoid hurrying or quick changes of activity or subject.
5. Do not condescend or talk 'across' them. Involve them in everything you say and do.
6. Never scold or humiliate or correct them. Remember their cognitive abilities are damaged. Your visit is meant to encourage and uplift them, not create turmoil or anxiety.
7. Do not feel obliged to challenge their version of reality. Research shows that as the condition progresses memories are gradually lost, beginning with the latest. It may be that the sufferer is living in a world that is in the past—but it is not an imagined world. They are not being delusional. Their world is very real, but it belongs to the past. They cannot comprehend the present 'reality' because of the brain damage.
8. Look for the meaning in what they say and do. Try to 'look beneath'. If someone is saying something

irrational, perhaps even 'gibberish', be respectful and try to read their body language.

9. Take everything one step at a time. Think 'linear'.

10. Focus on their remaining abilities, and do things in small steps.

11. Remember—keep it simple, keep it short and keep it sweet! Don't overload them with information or ideas.

12. Don't be afraid to repeat things, but do so gently, and with patience.

13. In coming to spiritual activity, such as praying, reading from the Bible or singing a hymn, tell them clearly what you are about to do. Repeat yourself gently if they wander off onto a different subject. Tell them what you are going to sing and try to get them to join in. You will have found out in advance what hymns or songs are relevant to them. We all love our old favourites, and when you have dementia these old favourites are touchstones for happy memories and feelings. Use the hymns and worship songs that are relevant to them.

14. Speak about reassuring things. Loss of assurance and loss of confidence in God are not unusual in frailty and confusion.

15. Encourage them from the Scriptures when they express guilt and fears. Make a note of Hebrews 13:5–6; 2 Timothy 2:19; Psalm 71:18; John 20:28–30; Psalm 103:13–14; Romans 8:28–30, 34–37.

16. There may be particular passages of Scripture or hymns that they will respond to more than others— don't worry about using them most of the time.

17. Draw on things they will know, for example, events of their childhood, Sunday School songs, familiar hymns and well-known Bible stories. Use pictures, photographs, or things that will remind them.

18. Speak frequently about Christ and the cross. Talk

gently rather than preach. Don't be aggressive! Remind them of the glories of heaven, using the Scriptures when you can: John 14:1–3; Revelation 21:3–5; 22:1–4; Jude 24. There are many more you probably know well.

19. If appropriate, hold the person's hand, or touch their arm from time to time. You will have found out in advance whether or not this is helpful.

20. It's always good to pray, briefly, at the end of your visit. Prayer brings calm and a sense of peace as the Holy Spirit ministers.

See the 'For Further Help and Information' section at the end of this book for a list of books by Louise Morse.

APPENDIX 4. JAMES 5:14–16: HEALING AND CHURCH ELDERS

There are fewer subjects in the church with the potential to promote disagreement and division than that of healing. Some, in their caution, prefer to ignore the possibility of healing altogether, and in their visiting of the sick will pray for anything and everything but. Yet there is the danger that those of us at the cautious end of the spectrum, while succeeding in avoiding unhelpful extremes and in raising unrealistic hopes, stand in danger of 'throwing the baby out with the bathwater', thereby failing to obey that which is clearly given in Scripture in this realm. Undoubtedly this passage in James may, frustratingly, not be as clear as we would wish. But bearing in mind that normally 'the main things are the plain things, and the plain things are the main things', let us state firstly those things that are clear in this important section of God's Word, and then consider the matters flowing from them.

The clear things in James 5:14–16

1. The healing mentioned here is placed firmly within the context of the local church.
2. It is the church elders who are to be called to pray for the sick person.
3. It is the responsibility of the sick person to take the initiative and call the elders requesting prayer for healing.
4. The elders are to anoint the sick person with oil.
5. The elders are to offer the prayer of faith.

Matters to consider flowing from these verses

1. JAMES MUST BE REFERRING TO AN EXTREME CASE OF SICKNESS IN A BELIEVER
The afflicted one seems to be confined to bed and needing to be 'prayed over' and 'raised up' (vv. 14–15).

2. IT IS POSSIBLE THAT THERE IS SIN TO BE CONFESSED AND REPENTED OF

This implies that sin in the fellowship (e.g. division, anger, bitterness, jealousy, resentment) can have physical as well as spiritual consequences. (Paul mentions the dire consequences of certain unconfessed sin in 1 Cor. 11:30.) It is certainly *not* the case that sickness is always a result of sin. But if by any chance it is ('*If* he has sinned', v. 15), the sin may be confessed and physical healing may be granted.

3. THE ANOINTING WITH OIL IS UNDOUBTEDLY OF SYMBOLICAL SIGNIFICANCE

If the oil had medicinal qualities, it would not necessitate the calling in of the elders; anyone could apply the healing oil. It therefore seems to symbolize the Holy Spirit's healing presence, or even the ministry of consecration by which individuals were singled out for anointing (1 Sam. 16:13; Isa. 61:1; Acts 4:27).

4. THE PRAYER OF FAITH PERHAPS RAISES THE BIGGEST QUESTION

Whose faith is it that is required—the sick person's or that of the elders? It simply is not clear; but what *is* clear is the *kind* of faith that is called for here. It is that Spirit-wrought conviction that God is in this and intends to raise up the sick person. It is a 'given' faith: a 'faith for the occasion' which will prove to be according to God's will because it came directly from God and therefore will be effectual (1 John 5:14–15).

5. ENCOURAGEMENT IS GIVEN TO THE RELUCTANT

Most of us would approach this scenario with a deep feeling of unworthiness, yet James selects that great Old Testament man of faith, Elijah, and encourages us by saying that he 'was a man just like us' (v. 17)—a sinner dependent upon the grace and righteousness of God. This godly hero battled with fear, doubt and depression—but he prayed earnestly (vv. 17–18). So elders, go in confidence, assured that you are clothed in the spotless righteousness which only Christ can provide.

6. THIS IS CLEARLY A GRACIOUS PROVISION OF THE POSSIBILITY OF HEALING

God has placed it within the 'safe environs' of the local church where the afflicted one is known and loved by Christ's under-shepherds. They have no need to coldly dissect and fully understand this passage before seeking to administer healing, but rather, moved with the same deep compassion that burns in their Saviour's heart, they go in his name—despite any dark doubts—with the earnest desire to see this beloved one raised up and restored in every way.

Pride and prejudice

Let us ensure that we who proudly succeed in avoiding the pitfalls of the 'extremists' are careful to avoid sinking in the quicksand of unbelief, thereby depriving many a sufferer of relief that could have been provided through godly, caring local-church elders. There is enough clear truth in these verses to give us confidence to seek healing for the afflicted brother or sister upon request, but sufficient ambiguity to guard us from any unhelpful dogmatism.

FOR FURTHER HELP AND INFORMATION

Pastoral visiting

Richard Baxter, *The Reformed Pastor* (Edinburgh: Banner of Truth, 1981)

Andrew Bonar, *Memoir and Remains of Robert Murray M'Cheyne* (Edinburgh: Banner of Truth, 1978)

Derek J. Prime and Alistair Begg, *On Being a Pastor: Understanding Our Calling and Work* (Chicago: Moody, 2004)

Mental health issues

Jim Winter, *Depression: A Rescue Plan* (Epsom: Day One, 2000)

The following helpful websites or pages also signpost to other resources:

- Eating disorders: A New Name by Emma Scrivener, http://emmascrivener.net/
- CBT and Christians: Christ the Truth by Glen Scrivener, https://christthetruth.wordpress.com/2010/05/01/cbt-from-a-christian-perspective/
- The son of Rick and Kay Warren tragically took his own life. They have a deep desire to be of help to the church generally on mental health issues. See their helpful Resources page at http://mentalhealthandthechurch.com/

Dementia/Alzheimer's

Books by Louise Morse:

Could It Be Dementia? Losing Your Mind Doesn't Mean Losing Your Soul (Oxford: Monarch, 2008)

Dementia: Frank and Linda's Story: New Understanding, New Approaches, New Hope (Oxford: Monarch, 2010).

Worshipping with Dementia: Meditations, Scriptures and Prayers for Sufferers and Carers (Oxford: Monarch, 2010).

ENDNOTES

Introduction

1 Warren W. Wiersbe, *On Being a Servant of God* (Nashville: Thomas Nelson, 1993), p. 3.

Chapter 1

1 Andrew Bonar, *Memoir and Remains of Robert Murray M'Cheyne* (Edinburgh: Banner of Truth, 1978), p. 56.

2 James L. Snyder, *The Life of A. W. Tozer: In Pursuit of God* (Camp Hill, PA: Christian Publications, 1991), p. 211.

3 C. S. Lewis, *The Problem of Pain* (Kindle edn.; London: Centenary Press [no date]), p. 41.

4 Richard Dawkins, Twitter post, 20 August 2014, https://twitter.com/richarddawkins/status/502106262088466432, accessed 27 August 2015.

Chapter 2

1 R. Harvard MD, Appendix to Lewis, *The Problem of Pain*.

2 Roger Carswell, 'Treasures of Darkness: Depression—A Personal Point of View', at Tell Me More, http://tell-me-more.org, accessed August 2015.

3 Personal correspondence, March 2105.

4 Ibid.

5 Billy Graham, *Nearing Home: Life, Faith, and Finishing Well* (Nashville: Thomas Nelson, 2011), p. vii.

Chapter 4

1 John Ross, 'Robert M'Cheyne: A Model of Manly Ministry', Recycled Missionaries blog, 22 May 2013, https://johnstuartross.wordpress.com. (Originally published in *The Record*, the magazine of the Free Church of Scotland.)

2 Bonar, *Memoir and Remains of Robert Murray M'Cheyne*, p. 58.

3 I. D. E. Thomas, *A Puritan Golden Treasury* (Carlisle, PA: Banner of Truth, 2000), p. 66.

4 From Bible Truth Publishers, bibletruthpublishers.com.

Chapter 5

1 B. A. Ramsbottom, *Christmas Evans* ([n.p.]: Gospel Standard, 1985), p. 52.

Chapter 6

1 Joni Eareckson Tada, *A Place of Healing: Wrestling with the Mysteries of Suffering, Pain, and God's Sovereignty* (Colorado Springs, CO: David C. Cook / Eastbourne: Kingsway, 2010), p. 48.

2 Ibid., p. 42.

3 Quoted in Thomas Watson, *All Things for Good* (Edinburgh: Banner of Truth, 1986), p. 25.

Chapter 9

1 Jonathan Edwards, *Heaven: A World of Love* (Pocket Puritan Series; Edinburgh: Banner of Truth, 2008); taken from Charity and Its Fruits, Sermon 16 on 1 Cor. 13:8–10.

2 Joni Eareckson Tada and Jack S. Oppenhuizen, *Hidden and Forgotten People: Ministry Among People with Disabilities*, Section 4b and 4c of

Lausanne Occasional Paper No. 35B, 2004; at lausanne.org.

Appendix 1

1   From Carl F. George, *Prepare Your Church for the Future* (Tarrytown, NY: Revell, 1991), pp. 129–131.

Appendix 3

1   Taken from Louise Morse and Roger Hitchings, *How to Help Dementia Sufferers* (Pilgrim Homes), www. pilgrimsfriend.org.uk. Louise Morse is a journalist with a diploma in international marketing and a Masters in Cognitive Behavioural Therapy. Passionate about the well-being of older people, she is Media and Communications Manager for the Pilgrims' Friend Society.